READY, AIM, FIRE!
The Real Adventures
of Annie Oakley

READY, AIM, FIRE!
The Real Adventures of Annie Oakley

Ellen Levine

SCHOLASTIC INC.
New York Toronto London Auckland Sydney

Photo and Art Credits
ii: Buffalo Bill Historical Center (Cody, Wyoming) • **26, 32, 42, 88-89 and 99:** Illustration by John Monteleone • **23:** Ohio Historical Center (Columbus) • **49:** Notman Photographic Archives, McCord Museum, McGill University (Montreal) • **56:** Circus World Museum (Baraboo, Wisconsin) reproduced by permission of Ringling Bros.—Barnum & Bailey Combined Shows, Inc. • **93:** Western History Collections, University of Oklahoma (Norman) • **102:** Buffalo Bill Historical Center (Cody, Wyoming) • **114-115 and 126:** Garst Museum (Greenville, Ohio).

ISBN 0-590-41877-7

Copyright © 1989 by Ellen Levine. All rights reserved.
Published by Scholastic Inc.

12 11 10 9 8 7 6 5 4 3   9/8 0 1 2 3 4/9

Printed in the U.S.A.   28

First Scholastic printing, July 1989

Acknowledgments

Particular thanks to Paul Fees, Curator of the Buffalo Bill Museum, Buffalo Bill Historical Center, Cody, Wyoming; and Bess Edwards, President of the Annie Oakley Foundation, Royal Oak, Michigan, who were most generous with their time and knowledge. I am also grateful to Christina Stopka, Archivist/Librarian, and Joan Murra, Library Clerk, at the Buffalo Bill Historical Center; Shirl Kasper; Daniel Rich of Vathek Books, Fort Lee, New Jersey; and Toni Seiler, Director of the Garst Museum, Greenville, Ohio. I am especially indebted to Anne Koedt, Inger Koedt, and Bonnie Kreps, who recognized a good story and urged its telling.

In memory of
Myra Lipschutz and Miguel Marrero.

Chapter One

"**W**hat are you staring at, Annie?" John asked as he looked up from sweeping the cinders into the fireplace.

Annie sat crosslegged on a chair. She didn't answer at first. John broke into her silence again. "What are you looking at?"

"That gun," Annie said, pointing to the rifle hanging over the fireplace. John turned to look up at the dusty rifle. Lacy threads of a large cobweb wound from the trigger to the wall behind.

"That gun was Papa's," Annie said, "and nobody's used it since he died."

"Haven't had much meat since then, either," John added.

"You know what?" Annie jumped up. "I'm going hunting!"

"But you don't know how to shoot," John said.

"I'm picturing Papa," said Annie, as she climbed up on a chair and reached for the rifle. She handed it down to John and, with the powder horn and shot bag in her hands, she jumped to the floor. Annie Moses was eight years old and her brother John just five.

"I wish I could remember Papa," murmured John.

"You were too little when he died," Annie said. "Only three."

Jacob and Susan Moses, Annie's parents, had built a log cabin in the little township of North Star, Ohio. With a household of seven children, they had farmed the new land. But in the chill of the winter of 1866, Jacob Moses had died. Within a year, the oldest daughter, Mary Jane, had caught pneumonia and was buried next to him.

Susan Moses and the rest of the children tried to work the farm, but the earnings were small. When their supplies were nearly gone, Mrs. Moses took a job as a community nurse, often traveling away from home for days at a time.

On this spring morning in 1869 Annie and John

2

were alone, for Mrs. Moses was on a nursing trip and their older sisters had taken baby Hulda to a neighbor's house.

"Hold this," Annie said as she handed John the little bag.

"What's in here?" John asked.

"Shot," Annie said. "Bullets. They go down the gun, but first I have to put in this powder." She picked up the horn and poured the powder into the barrel. She wasn't sure how much she needed, so she used all of it. Then she took a bullet and shoved it down on top of the powder.

"Now we have to push down with this ramrod," she explained to John, using the long wooden stick that was hooked to the rifle.

Annie pushed and pulled, and by the time she was finished, she was covered with grease, dust, and bits of powder — and so was John.

"Let's go!" Annie cried as she ran out of the cabin toward the pasture. She climbed up the fence and rested the rifle barrel on the top bar. Just then a fat squirrel darted across the field.

"Stand back, John," Annie whispered. "It's going to be squirrel pie for supper tonight!" She cocked the lock and pulled the trigger.

BANG!

The next thing Annie knew, she was sprawled on the ground. The squirrel raced wildly into the woods.

Annie hadn't expected such an explosion. Red-faced and a little bruised on her nose and chin, she picked herself up and wiped the dirt off her clothes. John watched silently as she reached for the rifle. "I guess I put in a little too much powder," she said sheepishly.

John nodded. "Probably enough to kill a cow," he said in an awed voice.

"Come on," Annie said. "We'd better clean up before Mama gets home."

But they missed some gunpowder on the floor in front of the fireplace, and Mrs. Moses was puzzled as she swept it up that night. She also saw the bruises on Annie's face, and noticed that the rifle was a little crooked on its pegs over the fireplace.

"What have thee been doing, Annie?" she asked. Annie's mother was the only one in the family who still kept the Quaker way of speaking.

Annie hesitated. She knew her mother didn't like firearms.

"I wanted to try the gun," she said at last. "I was hoping to shoot us some game for supper."

Her mother looked quietly at her, finally reaching to smooth down Annie's hair.

"Annie, the next time thee feels thee must have the gun, ask me to help thee and thee'll not spill so much powder."

That night in bed, Annie was too excited to sleep. Come morning she'd ask her mother for help. "Next time," she whispered to herself, "I won't miss!"

Chapter Two

Annie practiced her shooting, and before long she was bringing game home for supper. But times weren't easy on the Ohio frontier. A drought or a sudden chill could wipe out a farm family's crop.

Hard as she tried, Susan Moses couldn't keep the land. She had to sell most of the furniture and the cow and move with her children to a smaller home. She married again, and soon Annie had another little sister, Emily. Still things did not go well. Families like Annie's struggled through these years, sometimes receiving help from friends.

Neighbors offered to take care of little Hulda. Although she was grateful for their kindness,

Annie's mother wanted to keep all her children at home. But at last, desperately poor, she accepted, and Hulda went to live with the Bartholmews.

One night as Annie's mother put away her sewing, she motioned to Annie to sit beside her.

"I saw Mrs. Edington today at the market," she began. Annie knew Mrs. Edington was the matron of the Darke County Infirmary, the local home for orphans, mentally ill people, and others too poor, too sick, or too old to take care of themselves. "She said thee could stay with her for awhile."

Annie caught her breath. Live in the poorhouse . . . alone. . . !

"For how long?" she asked.

"Not long. A few weeks . . . a month, perhaps. Until we have a little more money." Annie's mother paused and took Annie's hands. "Mrs. Edington promises to teach thee fancy stitches."

Annie pulled back. "But Mama, Hulda is with the Bartholmews, and Lydia is married. It's just me and John and Emily and Elizabeth and Sarah Ellen with you. I'll work harder, I promise!"

Her mother looked away and said softly, "Thee will be better off in the home in these hard times." She paused and then continued, "Mrs. Edington is coming tomorrow."

7

And so at age nine, Annie went to live at the county poorhouse.

People came and went in the poorhouse, some quickly, some staying for years. Always there was a need for new or mended clothes, and Annie learned to sew. Mrs. Edington was a good teacher and Annie was a quick and careful learner. Annie had loved to spend hours in the woods. Sewing meant staying indoors, but if she had to sew, she'd do it well. Each stitch she made was small and tight and neat and just like the one before it.

For months, Annie spent her days sewing, cleaning, and helping with whatever Mrs. Edington needed. Then one day everything changed for Annie. A well-dressed man drove his carriage up to the poorhouse door and went into Mrs. Edington's office.

He introduced himself and said, "My wife and I have just had a baby, and we would like a young girl to live with us as a mother's helper. Would this be possible?"

Mrs. Edington nodded. It was not an unusual request. She was always pleased when she could find a good home for one of her girls. The gentleman said he had a large farm not far from the home and made enough money to pay fifty cents a week for help. He also promised to send the young girl to school, paying for all the costs of her education.

"I think I have just the girl for you," said Mrs. Edington. "Wait here a moment, will you?"

As she walked to the sewing room, Mrs. Edington was working out a plan.

"Annie dear, come over here." Annie sat down next to Mrs. Edington on a bench by the window. "Would you like to help with a little baby and go to school and earn some money in the bargain?"

Annie had helped care for her baby sisters, but school and earning money — that was something new. This was a chance to send money home, and, at the same time, a chance to learn to read and write!

Annie had never been to school. School was not free in the 1860s in Ohio. And besides, Annie's family lived too far for the children to walk to the schoolhouse. All she knew was the alphabet. She quickly nodded yes, too excited to ask how this miracle was to happen.

"I'll have to write to your mother for permission," Mrs. Edington said. "But I'm sure she'll agree. Come now and meet the gentleman who wants to take you to his home." As they walked to the office, Mrs. Edington explained about the family and what the man had promised to do.

That night in bed, Annie kept seeing the letters of the alphabet dancing on the ceiling beams. Soon they'll be words, lots of long, fancy words, she said to herself happily. Annie had always loved to look at and touch the family Bible. Her father and mother had written the family's births and deaths on the inside cover. She used to trace the letters with her finger, wishing she could read the words. Soon, she thought, as she drifted off to sleep.

Chapter Three

Mrs. Edington wrote promptly to Annie's mother. When the letter came back saying "Yes," Annie couldn't believe she could feel so happy. The gentleman came one afternoon, and Annie rode off with him, certain that whatever happened would be wonderful.

Never in her nine years of life had she been so wrong.

"You will rise at four A.M. to prepare breakfast," the man's wife said. "Biscuits, fried cornmeal mush, bacon, potatoes, and coffee."

"Then you will milk the cows and feed the pigs," the man added.

"And wash the dishes, do the laundry, pick the vegetables for dinner, and rock the baby to sleep." The woman seemed pleased as she kept adding to the list of Annie's duties.

"My schoolbooks, sir?" Annie asked the man. He looked away as he answered.

"We will see about that."

Weeks later Annie was given an old school speller and copy book. She propped the speller up behind the sink as she washed the dishes. But the woman caught her and grabbed the book, tossed it on the floor and shouted at Annie to mind her work. The same thing happened every time Annie tried to look at her books.

These people are like wolves in sheep's clothing, Annie thought. They fool you at first — they seem so gentle — but they are dangerous.

And that's what Annie called the man and the woman — the wolves. She thought of them as Mr. and Mrs. wolf, but never with a capital w, for that would make it like a real name. She vowed never to say their real name to herself or anyone else. And she never did.

Then something surprising happened. Mr. wolf told her she'd be sent to school for a few weeks. She didn't ask why, for she talked as little as possible in this house. She just nodded. But alone in her room she slowly let herself feel a growing excitement.

Annie's happiness didn't last long. The other children at the school found out she had come from the poorhouse. They teased her, making fun of her clothes, her ignorance, and most of all, her name.

"Moses Poses — wish she'd smell like roses!"

"Moses, Holy Moses, got any new tablets to-day?"

"It's the Moses kid . . . born in the bull-rushes . . . floating on a leaf. . . ."

"Moses, Moses, stuck up noses. . . ."

Annie yelled back, and sometimes got into fights. But the teasing never stopped, and Annie was almost relieved when the wolves told her she couldn't go anymore. She hadn't learned much about reading and writing at the school, but she had learned to hate her name. Someday, she said to herself, I'm going to change my name.

At the farm Annie's day again began before dawn and often ended near midnight. One night as she sat mending stockings, her eyes began to close and her head tipped forward as she started to fall asleep over the pile of sewing. A sharp slap brought her to her feet, her eyes stinging with tears of pain.

"Sleep, will you, when there's work to be done? Not in this house!" the wolf woman shrieked. It was not the first time Annie had been struck by one of the wolves, and it was not the last.

Chapter Four

Months passed and Annie longed to go home to her mother and brother and sisters. One night she went into the sitting room to speak to the woman.

"Ma'am, may I go to visit my mother? It would only be for a few days and I'd so love to," she said.

Mrs. wolf laughed hoarsely. "No! And if you ask again, I will cut out your liver and heart and hang them on the fence for the crows to eat!"

Annie didn't ask again.

Two winters passed, and still she cooked and cleaned for the wolves and the other animals on the farm. She couldn't even write a letter to her mother, for she didn't know how.

Late one afternoon Mr. wolf came home from

town with supplies and the mail. Annie saw that one of the envelopes had her name on it. Mrs. wolf snatched it up quickly from the table and read it to herself. She looked up at Annie and said, "Your mother says everything is fine at home and that she is pleased you are staying with us." Then as Annie reached for the letter, the woman walked to the wood stove and tossed the sheet of paper into the fire. "Oh, I'm sorry," she turned and said sarcastically. "Did you want to keep it?"

At last one spring day the man and woman took the baby and went on a two-week trip.

"When we return," Mr. wolf told Annie, "you may visit with your mother." Annie could hardly wait.

On their first night back, Annie asked when she could go home. The woman just stared at her as if she were speaking in a foreign language. Then she continued knitting. Annie turned to the man. "But . . . you promised. . . ."

"Stop whining, girl!" he hissed. "Don't you dare speak about going home again!"

How could I have believed them? Annie thought. She wouldn't make the same mistake again.

One morning the wolves told Annie they were taking the baby on a day trip. As their carriage drove away, Annie planned her escape.

She carefully went about her chores. She fed and watered the animals, cleaned the sink, changed the linens, and ironed a pile of clothing, which she left neatly folded on the kitchen table.

Then she wrapped her few things in a cloth, and without a glance back walked hurriedly toward the nearby town and railroad station. She was headed toward Greenville and climbed aboard the first train going in that direction.

The old gentleman looked up from his newspaper as Annie sat down in the empty seat next to him. "How do you do, little Miss?" he said.

Annie was not used to telling strangers her troubles, but the man had such a pleasant face, and she had not talked with anyone except the wolves for so long. Before ten minutes had passed, he knew that Annie had worked for a family that had not treated her well and that she was at last on her way to see her mother after two years. He also knew that she had no money.

When the conductor came to collect the tickets, the old man offered to pay Annie's fare. The conductor listened to a small part of Annie's story. Then he pursed his lips, scratched his head, and paused. "Free pass," he said and walked off.

Many miles and many hours later, Annie finally arrived home. She was so happy to see her mother, brother, and her little sister, who had grown so much in the two years Annie had been away. But her mother was once again a widow, for Annie's stepfather had died. Annie also learned that the evil of the wolves had a long reach.

"I wrote asking that thee be sent home, for we needed thee here," her mother said when they were at last alone. She looked up from her sewing as she continued. "But they wrote to me saying thee didn't wish to come home, that thee wished to stay in school."

Annie couldn't believe her ears. "Mama, I never knew," she said with a gasp. "They told me you wanted me to stay there. And most of the time I wasn't even in school. . . . I wanted so to come home," she cried, "but they wouldn't let me!"

Her mother put down her sewing and opened her arms wide. Annie ran to her.

Chapter Five

It was wonderful to be home and to rediscover her woods. Annie wandered the hills and forests, and slowly began to feel happy again.

As often as she could, Annie went hunting. One morning, she pulled an empty burlap sack over her clothing to protect against burrs and thorns. Hefting her shotgun over one shoulder and her powder horn and shot bag over the other, she made her way across streams, pushing through underbrush, looking for game.

Suddenly there was a flapping of wings as a quail flew out of the brush. Annie whirled around, gripping the shotgun in both hands. Before she shot, she spun around twice, and only then brought the gun to eye level and fired.

Annie never shot sitting game. It was too easy. Besides, it didn't give them a fair chance, she said. She kept pushing herself to become faster and faster, until she didn't think about sighting and aiming at her target. She did it as naturally as tying her shoe. The gun was part of her arm, part of her eye, part of herself.

Annie had a new stepfather, Joseph Shaw. Little Emily called him Grandpap Shaw, and so did everyone else. Grandpap Shaw was a mail carrier traveling to and from Greenville and the smaller towns and villages in the county. At one time he had been rich, but he had lost almost everything in a bad business deal. He and Annie's mother and the children were starting over again.

Grandpap Shaw had had just enough money left to build a new log cabin. It was large, with two stories, and two rooms on each floor. He was a gentle and kind man, but not wise about money. He had had to borrow from the bank, and now he couldn't make the monthly payments on the loan.

"Grandpap," Annie said one day, "I've been thinking. Charlie Katzenberger in town says he'll buy birds from me, as many as I can shoot. But you'll have to deliver them for me."

"You mean on my mail trips?" the old man asked.

She nodded. "I've got some ready if you'll take them tomorrow."

And with that, Annie began to earn money on a regular basis.

Sometimes she went in with Grandpap Shaw and delivered her game in person. Greenville was the biggest town Annie had ever seen. In the woods, she could spend a whole day alone. In town, people jostled each other on the crowded main street. And the noise! The sawmill and flour mills ripped and ground, it seemed, all day and night. Trains pulled in and out of the station at least twice a day.

In Charlie Katzenberger's General Store the noises were friendly. Customers examined goods, argued over prices, gossiped with neighbors, or just passed the time of day.

Charlie Katzenberger knew well-shot game when he saw it. He shipped most of Annie's birds to the big hotels in Cincinnati, eighty miles away. There the manager of the prestigious Bevis Hotel, Jack Frost, bought as much as he could. Unlike many hunters in those days, Annie shot birds cleanly through the head. Bevis Hotel customers never bit down on shot pellets during dinner. Mr. Frost didn't yet know the name Annie Moses, but anything from Charlie Katzenberger was welcome.

When she went to Greenville, Annie also spent time in Frenchy LaMotte's store. Frenchy had come to America many years before, but he still spoke with a rich accent. He'd been a trapper in the western mountains, and with that knowledge he traded skins and sold traps, guns, ammunition, and anything else a hunter might need.

"Ah, Miz Mozee," he'd say in his deep voice. "What 'ave you for me today?"

Annie loved the way he said her name. It had a soft, musical sound. She'd smile and show him fox and mink and raccoon skins.

Annie wasn't yet fourteen years old when she paid off the last note on the bank loan.

"It's done!" Grandpap Shaw announced one day after a trip to town. He put the paper marked "PAID" on the kitchen table. Annie's mother smiled quietly. Then she folded the paper carefully and put it away in the drawer that held all the important papers.

Annie helped feed and support her family by shooting game in a time when women were supposed to stay home, sew, cook, and clean.

That night the family celebrated with a feast of Annie's game.

"It's a miracle the way you shoot, my girl," said Grandpap Shaw as he beamed at Annie.

"And I remember how she started," said her brother, John, with a laugh.

Chapter Six

Annie kept on selling game to Charlie Katzenberger, and with her earnings the family built a
springhouse, a separate little building to keep milk
cool in summer and apples and potatoes stored
for winter.

Annie and her mother shared a love for fruit
trees. They planted apple and pear, and couldn't
wait for the sweet smell of the spring blossoms.
It pleased Annie deeply to take care of herself and
help her family.

Every now and then, people from the neigh-
boring farms and townships gathered in an open
field for a shooting match. Boys and their fathers
oiled their guns and lined up to take aim at a

distant nail head mounted on a target.

"Hit the nail on the head and take a turkey home for dinner," the announcer would sing out. Annie was almost always the only girl to enter the contest.

"I'm not shooting against any girl," one young boy sneered.

"Me neither!" said his friend. "Besides, what do girls know about shooting?" he said. "Who is she, anyway?" he asked his friend.

Annie was loading her gun. "I'm Annie Mozee," she said quietly. *Annie Mozee*, she thought to herself. It had slipped out before she knew it. Well, it's nicer than Moses, she decided. From now on, I'm Annie Mozee.

The chattering of the men and boys brought her attention quickly back to the match.

"Would you like to stand a step or two closer?" one of the men asked, smiling at her. "We wouldn't want to take advantage of you!" The boys snickered.

Annie said, "No, thank you," and stepped to the firing line. When it was her turn to shoot, the whispers started again. And then stopped suddenly.

"Hit the nail on the head! The winner, Miss Annie Mozee!" shouted the announcer.

"Must have been an accident," said the boy who hadn't wanted to shoot against a girl.

"Yeah," muttered his friend.

But after half a dozen shooting meets, the men and the boys weren't chuckling anymore. With respect, and sometimes a little irritation, they'd move aside when it was Annie's turn. Then one day, they'd had enough.

"It's no match when you're shooting," one said to her. "We all know who's going to win." They decided then and there, no more turkey shoots for little Annie Mozee.

Chapter Seven

When she was fifteen years old, Annie was invited by her older sister Lydia to stay with her in Cincinnati. Lydia had been happy to leave the farm after she married Joseph Stein. North Star, thought Lydia, was nowhere, and her sister Annie should have a chance to see what Lydia thought was "real" life — the big city.

Cincinnati in 1875 was a bustling river town. Hotels, restaurants, theaters, and shooting galleries lined the downtown streets. Joseph Stein enjoyed showing off Annie's shooting skills. One day he took her to a gallery owned by Charles Stuttelberg.

"The Bevis Hotel buys that girl's fresh-shot

game," he announced proudly, as Annie hit target after target without a miss.

Stuttelberg was impressed. He belonged to the same shooting club as Jack Frost, the Bevis Hotel manager. Many's the time he'd heard Frost talk about the hampers of cleanly shot game. He couldn't wait to tell Frost that his shooter was in town.

At about this time, Frank Butler of the Butler & Company shooting team was checked in at the Bevis Hotel. Butler was a well-known sharp-shooter, who was performing in Cincinnati theaters. When he wasn't performing, he enjoyed the challenge of a match against a local celebrity. Jack Frost knew Butler's reputation. When Frost learned that his skilled game shooter was in town, he had an idea.

"I've got a match for you, Frank," he told the hotel guest one night. "A hundred dollars says my shooter can beat you."

"Who is he?"

"Oh, just someone from up country . . . not a name you'd know," Frost continued, " . . . but one who'll beat the socks off you!"

"Really!" said Frank. "If it's not Captain Bogardus or Dr. Carver, you've got yourself a bet. They're the only men I know who I'd bet on over me."

"Neither one," answered Frost, smiling as he thought of the young girl, barely five feet tall with two braids down her back.

"No sir, " he repeated. "Neither one of them."

A match was set for Thanksgiving day. Joe Stein checked with Annie.

"Sure!" was her quick reply. She was happy at any chance to shoot.

The day arrived, and that's when Annie learned she was to shoot against a famous performer. Perhaps she had been too quick to say yes, she thought nervously.

Frank looked around trying to spot his opponent. When he saw Annie in her homemade gingham dress standing by the gun table, he turned to Frost. "Who's the country girl?" he asked.

"That's your opponent," answered Frost. Frank's mouth fell open. Then he smiled. This, he thought, will be a tale for the telling! He tipped his hat to Annie as he approached the table.

"Are you ready?" called the announcer. Annie nodded. Frank sang out, "Yes!"

Frank had the first shot.

"Pull!" shouted the announcer, and the pigeon trap flew open. "Hit!" was the cry as the bird fell to the ground.

Annie had never shot at game released from a

trap. Her arms felt so heavy she wasn't sure she could swing the gun.

"She can't do anything against Frank Butler," she heard someone whisper.

"Don't know about that," came a reply. Well, Annie knew.

"Pull!" said the announcer. "Hit!" he added almost as quickly.

Back and forth Annie and Frank went. Then each missed one shot. Bird number twenty-five, the last, was released for Frank.

"Miss!" and the crowd became silent. Annie stepped up.

"Pull!"

A sudden smell of the woods, the wings dipping and swooping, Annie's eye and arm dipping and swooping.

"Hit!"

She'd won! Her first match against a professional and she'd won! Annie was dazed as she turned to Butler. He tipped his hat again and smiled as he shook her hand. Then he walked up to Jack Frost. "Here's your money, Jack," he said as he handed him a roll of bills. Looking back at Annie he murmured, "That little girl is one heck of a shot!"

Chapter Eight

Frank Butler was indeed a gracious loser. In fact, he hadn't really lost at all, he told friends. And in a way he was right. In the days and weeks after the match, Frank visited Annie at her sister's home. They went to the theater to see his act and afterwards to downtown restaurants.

Annie was fascinated by the trick shots Frank and his partner performed. She wanted to know if the glass balls were difficult to toss to exactly the right height, if Frank was afraid when he held up a playing card as a target, and most of all how he had trained his dog George to sit still with an apple as a target on his head.

Sometimes Annie and Frank sat on the porch

of Lydia's home talking well into the night. Before they realized what was happening, they were spending every free moment together. When Frank and his company were ready to leave Cincinnati, he and Annie walked and talked for hours. He promised he'd be back in a year's time.

On his return, Annie was the first person he visited. One day as they were walking, he turned and looked her straight in the eye.

"We'll have to be married," he said. Then he added, "That's the only way I'll get my hundred dollars back. . . !"

It took a little time to convince Annie's mother that marriage to Frank was a good idea.

"My dear, he's in show business. Nothing respectable about that," Annie's mother kept repeating. Many people in those days didn't think show business was a proper way to earn a living, and Susan Moses Shaw was one of them.

"But Mama, Frank doesn't drink or smoke or play cards. That must count for something," Annie insisted. And in fact it did. At last Mrs. Shaw accepted the idea and gave her approval.

Not too long after they were married, Frank was on the road again, and Annie went home to her mother's house in North Star. She was determined to conquer reading and writing this time. Every day she practiced using the family Bible, and wrote often to Frank of her progress.

Annie also practiced trick shots. She tried to copy some of the stunts Frank had performed, but with no volunteers to hold up objects, she worked instead with a fence post. Frank's dog, George, had sat patiently on stage with the apple on his head as Frank took aim and split the fruit into pieces. George would catch one of the pieces in his mouth before it hit the stage. Annie tried this with the farm dogs, but they wouldn't cooperate. Like Mrs. Shaw, they too didn't care much for show business.

It wasn't long before Annie had mastered most of the trick shots she'd seen. When Frank returned from a road trip, she decided to join him on the next tour rather than stay at home writing letters.

One spring morning in May, Annie, Frank, and Frank's partner, John Graham, arrived in Springfield, Ohio. The poster at the Crystal Hall Theater said, "Graham & Butler, Rifle Team and Champion All-Around Shots." It was a "specialty" act. They performed sharpshooting stunts in the theater between acts in a play. While stagehands changed the sets, Frank and John entertained the audience.

By early afternoon Frank was worried. John

had come down with a fever. By showtime it was clear he couldn't perform. Frank didn't dare cancel the show, for he and Annie needed the money.

"Can you do it, Annie?" Frank asked her. "You just have to hold the cards straight out, and I'll shoot through them. And you've watched John and me enough to know how to toss the glass balls. You've just got to get them high enough so that I can have time to aim and shoot."

"But Frank," she reminded him, "I can shoot as well as you. I think we should trade shot for shot. You shoot while I hold the card, and then you hold for me."

Not a bad idea! He wondered why he hadn't thought of it. Annie quickly prepared. She had no special costume to wear, just her ordinary clothes. They would have to do. She helped Frank unpack the rifles and revolvers backstage.

"Ladies and gentlemen. A change in our program this evening," the announcer said. "Mr. John Graham is ill. A young lady from the audience has kindly consented to take his place."

Annie listened in fascination. A *young lady from the audience*. . . . Well, technically she *was* from the audience, the audience backstage. Then through the curtain she heard the rustling and disgruntled murmurs from the audience. They'd paid their money for Graham and Butler. Who knew what they'd see now?

Annie stepped out from behind the curtain. As she and Frank took their places onstage, there wasn't much applause. Frank shot first. The audience warmed up. Then it was Annie's turn. This was the first time she had shot by artificial light. Frank tossed a ball in the air. Annie's shot was slightly off the mark. The audience groaned.

Then Frank tossed two balls. This time Annie was ready. She knew how much she'd been off, and she adjusted her sense of distance to the shadows cast by the lights.

Hit! And then hit again, and again. Annie split the playing card in Frank's hand to thunderous applause. She turned to face the audience with a little skip and kick. Smiling broadly, she and Frank bowed to their first success as a sharpshooting team.

Chapter Nine

"**B**utler and Butler" often performed four to six times a day, six days a week. When a show closed, they traveled by train to the next city, sometimes sitting up all night in a chugging, lurching railroad car. A new town, a new hotel, a few hours sleep, and then on to the next theater. It was tiring but exciting work, and Annie and Frank were happy working together.

The Butlers saved as much money as they could. Both of them had grown up poor. At age thirteen, Frank had worked for his passage on a sailing ship from Ireland to America. He had peeled potatoes, delivered milk on a pony cart, cleaned horses and their stables, sold newspapers, and trained dogs before he had become a sharpshooter. Although he and Annie were careful with their earnings, Annie had one regular expense. She always would take a little and send it to her mother.

"Mama will use it well," she said to Frank as she sat fixing a costume. Annie designed and sewed all her own outfits. They were attractive, but even more important, they were practical. She didn't use leather, for it was too heavy and hard to keep clean. And her dress tops and blouses were loose, so that she could swing her arms freely. She designed leggings that laced or buttoned up the side, and hemmed her skirts just below the knee, instead of ankle length like her everyday clothes. Long skirts got in the way of quick movement.

One day Frank came back to the hotel from a meeting with a booking agent. He looked discouraged.

"Seems some theater managers don't want family acts," he said, "unless it's with kids ages five to fifteen. What are we going to do?"

"You mean they won't take 'Butler and Butler'?" Annie asked, astonished.

Frank nodded, looking miserable. A few days later Annie came in from a walk, put up the teakettle, and turned to Frank.

"If they don't want a family act, we'll change the name. Butler and Oakley. That's what we'll be," she said with determination.

"Oakley?" Frank asked.

"Yes." And with that she turned to pour the tea.

No one knows for sure where the name Oakley came from. But once it became Annie's, it fit as if she'd been born with it.

Annie worked at conquering show business just as she'd worked at her sewing and reading — intensely, thoroughly, and with a sense of adventure. Frank was always coming up with new tricks for her to try. And Annie was always willing. She learned the arts of suspense and drama. The harder the shot seemed, the more the audience was intrigued. Annie would occasionally miss a shot on purpose. All the more of a thrill for the audience when she then succeeded.

Add the element of danger, and a simple shot would have the audience holding its breath. When Frank's dog George climbed onto his velvet cushion and Annie placed an apple on his head, a hush swept through the seats.

"That's theater," Frank would say, and Annie learned theater.

And so the three of them, Frank, Annie, and George, traveled through the Midwest, playing in

theaters in Ohio, Wisconsin, Michigan, Illinois, Indiana, and Minnesota.

One day Frank was contacted by the Sells Brothers, founders and managers of the largest traveling circus in America.

"It's an offer, Annie, to join their road show for a season that will last much of the year," Frank said.

Annie was excited. "Sells Brothers is a very big outfit. It'll be a chance to try something new and have a steady job at the same time. Let's do it."

Frank nodded happily. "Just what I was thinking," he said.

That first season, only Frank was a shooter. The

Sells wanted Annie to perform horseback-riding stunts with several other women. Pollie Lee juggled on horseback, Adelaide Cordona rode four horses at the same time, and Mildred Gardner was called the "Empress of the Sidesaddle." Annie would gallop around the arena standing in the saddle, or hang over the side, feet hooked in a stirrup, and pick up objects from the ground.

Annie was very particular about the saddles she used. Stunt riding was exhilarating but also dangerous. Each time before she rode she checked all the leather straps. Hanging down across the saddle, or swinging up one side and off the other while at full gallop, she depended on the strength of those straps. Whatever your work, Annie believed, your tools must be the best.

"I'm not riding with that saddle," she said one day to the circus manager. "The straps are frayed."

"Don't worry, Miss Oakley. The act looks good. Everything's been working just fine," came the answer.

"I'm talking about the saddle straps, not the act," Annie said, but the manager just smiled and chewed on his cigar. Annie walked over to her horse, put both hands on the saddle, and gave a sharp pull. The leather strap tore and the saddle fell to the ground.

"Everything's *not* just fine," she said as she walked away. The manager bit down hard on the cigar. The opening feature, the "Rose Garland," was about to start. Without Annie the riders wouldn't be able to perform the act.

"Cut the Garland," he growled to the program manager. The next day Annie had a new saddle.

Chapter Ten

The days were long, the work was strenuous, and Annie had a hard time living in a tent. She had gotten used to hotel living — changing rooms every few nights, making an anonymous room a home, comfortable and cozy, and then packing everything up a day or two later and moving on. But tents, with their canvas ceilings and walls, were harder for her. Little did she know she'd spend most of her life in a tent and brilliantly learn the art of living under canvas.

The long season ended in the late fall, and Frank and Annie began touring again as "Butler and Oakley, Premier Shots." In March, they opened at the Olympic Theater in St. Paul, Minnesota, and one night an unexpected visitor, a famous Indian chief, watched the show.

Sitting Bull — Tatanka Iyotake, as his people called him — was a chief and medicine man of the Hunkpapa Sioux. His people had once ranged across the Great Plains, their lands stretching as far as the eye could see. But pressed from all sides, the Indians had lost their lands to the white settlers. Then in 1876, the year Annie and Frank were married, the Sioux, with Sitting Bull as a leader, defeated the famed General Custer on the grassy hills of the Little Bighorn. Many whites called it a brutal massacre. A few said the Indians were defending their homes and land.

When more army troops were sent in, the Sioux at last were defeated. Many were rounded up and driven onto reservations. But Sitting Bull refused to go. Instead, he took his people to Canada. After four years, with supplies dwindling and little help from the Canadian government, he and the re-mainder of his people returned to the United States. He had been promised a pardon, but the promise was broken and he was put in jail. Two years later he went to the reservation at Standing Rock in the Dakota territory.

On a number of occasions, Sitting Bull was permitted to travel under guard with an army escort. One night during a trip to St. Paul, Sitting Bull decided to see the show at the Olympic Theater. When Butler and Oakley began to shoot, the old chief sat up and stared intently at Annie. He turned to the army major with him.

"I wish to meet this young woman whose sight is as sharp as an eagle's, this young woman whose grace reminds me of my daughter." The major knew that Sitting Bull had deeply loved this daughter who had died. The next day the major arranged to have Frank and Annie come to the hotel where he and Sitting Bull were staying.

When they arrived, the chief came into the room, looked closely at Annie, and spoke words she did not understand. She turned to an interpreter. "The chief says you have the good spirit in you. No one will ever harm you."

Sitting Bull, having lost one daughter, now wanted Annie to become a new daughter to him. Annie looked into the eyes of this tired but proud and strong man in front of her.

"Yes," she said, "I will be your new daughter."

Sitting Bull smiled and turned to his aides. One brought out the council pipe, which they all smoked. Then they danced and chanted.

Sitting Bull took Annie's hands and spoke again. *"Machin Chilla Watanya Cicilia."*

The interpreter translated, "My daughter, Little Sure Shot."

Chapter Eleven

For their 1884 season, the Sells Brothers decided to advertise both Frank and Annie as shooters. The posters proclaimed "Butler and Oakley, THE FAMOUS FAR WEST CHAMPION RIFLE SHOTS." Annie had never been west of Minnesota, but she had learned Frank's lesson well — "That's theater!"

In December the circus went south and set up in a big field in New Orleans. A World's Fair and Cotton Exposition was about to open, and the Sells thought the fair visitors would come to the circus as well.

The railroads offered cheap excursion tickets to the fair, expecting thousands to pour into the city. Instead, it was rain that poured in. Forty-four days of rain, nonstop. The tents sagged and dripped, the grounds were mud pools, the animals were miserable, and the performers weren't paid.

Another show had also hoped to take advantage of the World's Fair. Buffalo Bill's Rocky Mountain and Prairie Exhibition was camped in a nearby field. One soggy day Annie and Frank went to see the show. The dripping tents and the mud were all too familiar. But the show was completely different. There were Indian and cowboy performers, and masters at roping, riding, and shooting. This, however, was not a circus. Roping, riding, and shooting weren't trick acts. They were the actual skills of the Wild West.

William F. Cody, known as Buffalo Bill, had been a scout with the U.S. army during some of the Indian wars. He had seen herds of buffalo hurtling across the plains, and watched antelope leap at a gallop, so light they didn't seem to touch the ground. Audiences in the East were fascinated by stories of the West. And that's what Buffalo Bill and his partner, Nate Salsbury, intended to show them.

As Annie and Frank walked around, they were particularly impressed with the care and attention paid to the animals. The Indian ponies, the buffalo, the horses, and the elk were not, after all, props in this show. They were part of the story.

"Jimmy, do you think they'd hire us?" Jimmy was Annie's private name for Frank.

"Only one way to find out."

Major John Burke was Cody's general manager and press agent. He spoke with Annie and Frank.

"Well," he said, "nothing much happening now," as he nodded toward the rain. "What exactly is it that you do?"

Frank said, "My wife's the finest rifle shot in the country."

Burke smiled. "Well now, let's take a look."

They set up targets, found some glass balls, and loaded the guns. With her broad-brimmed hat protecting her face, Annie aimed and shattered the glass every time. Burke was smiling. "Lots of good publicity I could do about you, little Miss Oakley," he said. "But can't do any of it now. Besides, Cody and Salsbury aren't here. Why don't you come to see us in Louisville in the spring? We should be back on track then, and they can get a look at you."

It was a beautiful spring morning in Louisville when Frank and Annie found Nate Salsbury's tent. Salsbury set up an audition. Like Burke, he was very impressed.

"Captain Bogardus has left the show . . . " Captain Bogardus! Frank and Annie looked at each other. Bogardus was one of the top shooters in the country.

Salsbury continued, " . . . and we need someone who can perform as well. But I'm not sure we can pay you what you want." He paused. "I've an idea. Why don't you perform with the show for several days and we'll see how it goes."

Frank and Annie agreed. In less than forty minutes, Butler and Oakley had undergone another major change. This time, only Oakley would be shooting. Frank was proud of Annie's skills, and thought the act was better with just Annie.

"I'm a splendid manager, and why waste time shooting when you're so good by yourself?" He smiled at her. "Besides, I'd rather be working up new tricks."

The first night with the show, Buffalo Bill brought Annie and Frank to the food tent. Hundreds of performers and workers sat at long tables as waiters brought out platters piled high with food. Buffalo Bill called for everyone's attention.

He was a tall man with long hair to his shoulders. He wore a fringed leather jacket, a crimson shirt embroidered with prairie flowers, cream-colored trousers, and leather boots that were well above his knees. He took off his wide Stetson hat and pointed to Annie.

"This little Missy is Annie Oakley. She's going to be shooting with us, and I want you boys to welcome her and treat her well." From that day on, Annie was always "Missy" to Bill Cody.

A few months after Annie and Frank signed on, Major Burke went out to the Dakota territory to try to persuade Sitting Bull to join the show. The federal government had agreed to let him leave the reservation. The question was only whether the chief would agree.

Sitting Bull drove a hard bargain — he would appear for one season only at a good salary, and he would be the only one who had the right to sell his photos and autographs. He also made it clear he would never do anything to make his people look foolish or evil. Within weeks he was in a tent near his adopted daughter, Little Sure Shot.

When Sitting Bull appeared in the United States, the crowds hissed and booed him. In Philadelphia, a man asked him, "Don't you regret killing Custer and the American soldiers?"

Sitting Bull replied, "I have answered to my people for the Indians slain in that fight. The chief that sent Custer must answer to his people."

Annie enjoyed spending time with Sitting Bull. She had only read newspaper accounts written by white men about the battle of the Little Bighorn. Now she learned from Sitting Bull the Indians' side of the story.

The show traveled north to Canada that summer and then returned to the United States and toured until October when the season ended in St. Louis. The Buffalo Bill Wild West Show had been so successful, it had earned over one million dollars. And over a million people had seen it. Buffalo Bill was becoming very famous in show business, and so was Annie Oakley.

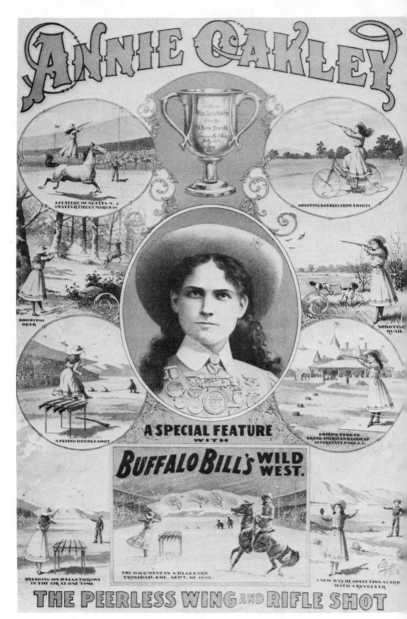

Annie performed with Buffalo Bill's Wild West Show for more than 16 years. This poster shows some highlights of her act.

Chapter Twelve

The Buffalo Bill Wild West Show was a traveling city, a whole neighborhood on the move. If Annie's horse needed a new shoe, there were several blacksmiths. If she needed repairs on her own shoes or boots, the shoemaker was only a few tents away. When Frank wanted his hair cut, the show barber did it. The seamstress made and fixed costumes for hundreds of performers, but not for Annie. She wanted to make her own.

There were bakers and cooks for all the show people, and also cooks who prepared food to sell to the audience. Carpenters built everything for the show, and if Annie needed her small tent table repaired, they helped out. Lighting experts prepared the gas lamps and in later years the big electric searchlights for night performances. In the ammunition wagon, staff loaded bullet shells every day for the performers, although Frank did Annie's. Both Frank and Annie were very particular about their guns. Frank cleaned and packed them so that they were like new. And every day he loaded her shells.

Some workers set up the tents, others the bleacher and grandstand seats for at least 15,000 people. Some took care of the animals, feeding and cleaning hundreds of horses, elk, buffalo, and moose.

About a month before opening in a new town, an advance team would arrive and make arrangements for all the necessary supplies. They would paste up thousands of posters on every available window, wall, and pole, announcing the arrival of the show.

The performers, animals, stage sets, props, and machinery filled more than two dozen railroad cars. When the Wild West train pulled in, it took hours to unload everything and set up in a baseball field, racetrack, park, or open field.

The cook tent was one of the first to go up. Almost immediately the huge pots and kettles were steaming and bubbling. After the tents were all up and a meal eaten, the public began to crowd the field. Show posters announced, "The West at your Doors! More Scouts! More skillful Marksmen and Markswomen! More Genuine Indians! More Western Animals! More Cowboys! More Wild Bucking Horses! The Largest Herd of Buffalo on the Continent!" The public was invited to come early and walk around the grounds, see the performers in their tents, watch the buffalo as they grazed and roamed their lot, buy souvenirs, munch on popcorn and soak up the feeling of the Wild West.

Annie watched the children as they gazed wide-eyed at everything. Many were poor, often without any adult with them. They clutched their pennies, hoping to have enough to get in to see the show. Annie often invited them in as her guests.

"Jimmy," she said one morning as she piled up their laundry. "Do you think the mother of one of these children would want a job washing and ironing?"

"Might be," he answered. He remembered how glad he was whenever he had been offered work in the early days.

One day Annie saw a little boy hanging around

the fence. She asked him if his mother took in laundry.

"Oh, yes!" he said quickly. Annie then asked him where he lived.

"Not far, not far at all," he answered even faster. Annie gathered up the bundle and the two started down the road. After awhile she said, "Are we almost there?"

"Oh, yes."

But on they walked.

Annie asked how much farther.

"Just down the road."

Miles later they reached his home. His grateful mother promised to return a cleaned and ironed pile in two days. Annie put her tired feet up when she got back to her tent.

One day Annie said to Cody, "Bill, there's an orphans' home in this town. You let all of them in free . . . " He waited as she paused, " . . . and I'll take care of the ice cream and candy!" That was the first of many "Orphans Days" at the Wild West Show.

Chapter Thirteen

"Ladies and Gentlemen, the Little Lass of the Western Plains, Champion Rifle Shooter, Little Sure Shot — The One and Only ANNIE OAKLEY!" A drumroll built to a loud roar. All eyes turned to the ring entrance as a young woman rode into the arena, jumped off her horse, and ran to a table with rifles.

Frank had entered with Annie. He tossed two glass balls into the air. The rifle whirled upward. Crack! and the glass shattered. Then he tossed six balls, one after another. Annie picked up one gun, shot two balls, then a second gun and shot two more, and then a third gun, and the remaining targets were shattered. Annie could feel the excitement building in the audience.

A mechanical trap released a clay pigeon that whirled and spun in the air. Annie was several yards from the gun table. She ran toward the table, leapt over it, picked up the rifle, aimed, and shot. The ceramic pieces scattered over the arena floor.

Then the shots became more daring. Frank held up a playing card and Annie put five or six holes in it. He turned the card sideways so that the edge faced her. Annie sliced the card in half. Then he held a dime between his fingertips. A single shot, and the dime had a hole dead center.

Another drumroll. People leaned forward in their seats. Slowly Frank took out a cigarette, lit it, and put it between his lips. He turned so that Annie faced his profile. She was thirty paces away from him. The audience became silent. Annie cocked her rifle and took careful aim. The ashes sailed off the tip of the cigarette. The audience went wild.

When Annie rode off, cowboys came in on bucking ponies. King of the Cowboys, Buck Taylor, led the group in riding and roping stunts. Then Buffalo Bill reenacted the story of his fight with the Indian warrior, Yellow Hand, and later rode in a buffalo hunt. The hoofbeats of the herd shook the stadium, and the dust flew as the big animals were chased around the arena and rounded up.

Annie and Frank watched from the side. A settlers' log cabin was set up in the middle of the arena. A woman was hanging laundry on the line. Several young children played in front of the cabin. A boy was chopping wood, and a man was returning home from hunting. Suddenly the air was filled with screams and hoofbeats. A troupe of Indians swooped down on the cabin, tomahawks raised, ready for a fight. Just when it seemed that the cabin would go up in flames and all the settlers would be killed, cowboys led by Buffalo Bill rode to the rescue, fought off the Indians, and saved the settlers.

In 1886 the Wild West Show opened in St. Louis, traveled through Indiana, Ohio, West Virginia, and Maryland, and then set up for a week in Washington, D.C. The show was even larger than the year before. More people, more animals, and more acts. Cody and Salsbury had added cowgirls who roped and rode bucking broncos with the cowboys.

During the last performance in Washington, Annie had felt a buzzing in her ear. When she finished her act, she and Frank went to their tent and he swabbed the painful ear. The next day Annie's ear still ached.

"I'm asking the doctor to have a look, Annie," Frank said. "Something's wrong. The swelling's getting bigger."

When the doctor arrived, he examined her and said that she had an insect sting. He assured them both that the swelling would go down soon.

But Annie didn't seem to get better, and Frank was worried. The show moved to Philadelphia. Annie had a fever and her ear was inflamed. Frank washed the ear again, and this time a tiny black insect came out.

"We've got the little villain," he said as he gently wiped Annie's forehead with a cold, wet cloth. "Everything's going to be fine now!" Annie nodded slowly. She had a fever and was exhausted. She fell asleep almost immediately.

The show moved to Staten Island in New York. For the first time, Buffalo Bill's Wild West was going to set up camp for the whole summer. On June 26, all the performers and some of the animals would board a ferry to Manhattan, parade through the streets of New York City, and then return to Staten Island. Thousands of people would see the parade. It was to be the grand introduction of the Wild West Show to New Yorkers.

Annie had made a new costume for the occasion. She had even stitched special harness drapings for her horse, but on parade day Annie sat in bed aching with fever.

"Jimmy, I've waited for months for this parade. I can't miss it!" she said.

"Please, Annie, you can't go. You're much too weak. It's only the parade. We'll be here all summer." But even as he said it, Frank knew it wasn't true. The parade was the beginning, a big beginning, and Annie was someone who was always in on things from start to finish. Still, he repeated, "Sweetheart, you can't go. You're just not well enough. Three hours on horseback through the streets of the city — it's just too much."

Annie listened and turned away. The time came for Frank to leave for the ferry. Annie lay in bed and watched him gather up his things. He said good-bye, but she looked away.

Ten minutes after everyone had headed for the dock, Annie swung her legs over the side of the bed, pulled the tent flap and yelled to an assistant nearby.

"Saddle my horse and bring him around front!"

Annie struggled into her costume and tilted her hat to cover the swollen side of her face. She mounted and rode to the ferry. Just as it was about to pull away, she raced up the gangplank to the cheers of the show people. Frank was stunned, but just put his arm around her as she leaned on his shoulder.

The parade was spectacular. Indians in war paint, cowboys swinging lassos in the air, Mexicans with wide sombreros, the Deadwood Stagecoach pulled by six mules, buffalo and longhorned steers filling the streets, and the whole parade headed by Buffalo Bill on his white horse with Annie not too far behind. An organ-grinder with his monkey got into the parade by mistake. But no one cared — the crowds cheered and whistled, applauded, and shouted hellos to all the performers.

Hours later back in her tent, Annie was burning with fever. She tossed in pain as the doctor examined her again.

"I'm afraid it's blood poisoning, Mr. Butler. An infection from the insect sting," he said.

Frank was white-faced. "How serious is it, doctor?"

"Very serious, I'm sorry to say."

Frank looked at Annie's face beaded with sweat. He turned back to the doctor.

"Will she make it?" he asked softly.

The doctor shook his head. "I don't know," he said. "I don't know."

Chapter Fourteen

For four days Annie hovered between life and death. She sweated, tossed about, moaned, and slept. Frank scarcely left her side. He wiped her down and changed her drenched bedclothes hour after hour. On the fifth day, she opened her eyes and murmured something he couldn't understand. But she was awake and cool to the touch! Then she leaned forward on one elbow and reached out to him. Frank took her hand and sat there without speaking.

Annie had been sick for four performances, the only time she would miss a show in the seventeen years she would perform with Buffalo Bill's Wild West. Although still a little weak, she was itching to get out of bed and begin again. She and Frank decided for the first few performances to eliminate some of the strenuous running and jumping stunts.

A little hesitant, a little nervous, she entered the ring for the first time in days. The glass balls still shattered, and the clay pigeons still burst into pieces after she pulled the trigger. The playing cards were once again riddled with holes. And the applause was once again wild. Annie Oakley was back!

All summer Buffalo Bill's Wild West played to huge crowds. Ferries left from Manhattan, Brooklyn, and New Jersey, almost nonstop, bringing thousands to the Staten Island show grounds every day for the three P.M. and eight P.M. performances.

One afternoon Mr. Henry Bergh came to see the show. Bergh was the head of the Society for the Prevention of Cruelty to Animals. He and several officers of the Society toured the grounds paying particular attention to the animal tents and feeding areas. Often circus animals were poorly treated, and some people had raised questions about the Wild West animals. There were so many animals, how could they possibly be taken care of properly?

Mr. Bergh took his seat in the stands and watched the show. A newspaper reporter recognized him and after the show rushed up, hoping for an exciting story with headlines screaming: "Buffalo Bill Bashes Beef! King of the West Brutal to His Namesakes!"

Instead Mr. Bergh was flushed with delight. "I am very pleased," he said. "The performance is very interesting and instructive. I have no fault to find with it in any way." Then he added, "I never saw so many real Indians together in my life, and they ride with great spirit and are very careful of their horses and other animals."

That night at a big barbecue feast after the evening show, Buffalo Bill announced the results. "A clean bill of health!" And Annie and Frank remembered how impressed they were when they first had seen the show animals two years earlier.

The summer season was so successful that Cody and Salsbury felt they could afford to rent Madison Square Garden for an entire winter season. They hired Steele MacKaye, a producer and dramatist, and Matt Morgan, a famous set designer, to create a spectacle on a scale never before seen.

The two men and their crews worked steadily for months, creating gigantic panoramas: mountains that seemed to reach the sky, stands of towering forests, the broad expanse of the high plains. They designed and built a special cyclone machine that sent gusts of wind powerful enough to drive the stagecoach halfway across the arena. As if by magic, Twenty-sixth Street and Madison Avenue in New York City was transformed into a mythical western frontier.

On Thanksgiving eve the show opened. Every seat in the Garden was filled. Buffalo Bill had added a new act, "Custer's Last Fight, the Battle of the Little Bighorn." The scene opened with Sioux Indians setting up their tepees in the middle of the arena and preparing for a war dance. Off to the side, hidden in a cluster of trees, a U.S. Cavalry scout watched. Then he disappeared and reemerged at General Custer's camp, where he told the general the location of the Indians. The soldiers mounted their horses and charged into the Indian camp. The Indians surrounded them and a fierce battle followed. Shots rang out, war whoops resounded, dust flew, and at last General Custer himself was killed. The Indians then retreated, leaving all the cavalry dead.

The lights dimmed in the arena, and in rode Buffalo Bill. A spotlight shone on him. He took off his hat as he paused over the body of General Custer. Behind him, the words "Too late!" appeared on a screen. And then, complete darkness. The silence was at last broken by thunderous applause.

The show played all through the winter months. One snowy night Annie and Frank were talking with Cody after the show. He pulled a letter from his pocket.

"Have a look at this, Missy," he said as he handed it to Annie. She took the thin tissue paper out of the envelope and read it.

"Oh, Jimmy," she said, turning to him. "It's from Mrs. Custer. She says she thought the show was wonderful, but she was so shaken after seeing the reenactment of her husband's death that she took to her bed the whole next day. Poor woman!" Annie murmured as she handed the letter back to Cody.

The three walked on in silence for a bit, heading for their hotel rooms. Suddenly Frank said, "Let's go get a bite to eat. I'm famished!" Stepping through the stage door, they saw a dark mass a few yards away. As they approached they realized it was a group of about twenty very poor men. They were huddled close together near the building wall, shivering.

Buffalo Bill, like Annie, had a soft spot for people in trouble. He reached into his pockets for some money, but found only a few coins. He turned to Frank.

"Butler, how much have you got with you?"

Frank opened his wallet and Annie her purse. Between them they scraped together twenty-five dollars.

"Lend it to me," Cody said to them. "I'll pay you back tomorrow."

Then he turned to the group and in a cheerful voice said, "Here boys, here's a dollar apiece. Go get a square meal and a bunk. It's too rough for a fellow to cruise around out here in the blizzard this night." With the few dollars still left, the three of them then went to dinner. Early the next morning Cody returned the money he had borrowed from Frank and Annie.

The show finally closed at the end of February. The famous author Mark Twain had been one of the frequent backstage visitors. Each time he had seen the show, he marveled at how realistic it was. Twain had traveled through the West during the frontier days.

"It brought back the breezy, wild life of the plains and the Rocky Mountains," he said. "Down to the smallest details the show is genuine!" Twain also suggested to Cody and Salsbury that they

**Annie Moses Butler and Frank Butler, about 1880. The Butlers were
married for almost fifty years.**

take the show to Europe. "It's time," he said, "that we send an exhibition that is purely and distinctly American." They agreed.

Annie was thrilled at the thought. Queens, kings, and dukes! London, Paris, Rome!

"Jimmy," she said one morning, "let's celebrate in advance. Let's go for a ride!"

It had snowed the night before and horsedrawn sleighs were gliding through the streets of the city. The street gaslights were still burning in the early morning hours. Annie and Frank headed for the Madison Square Garden stables. When they arrived, Annie walked right by the horses.

"Where are you going?" Frank asked. She kept on walking. When he caught up with her, she had stopped in front of Jerry, a large shaggy moose. Smiling mischievously she turned to Frank.

"Let's take a ride!" she repeated.

They harnessed Jerry to a sleigh and joined the traffic on the avenue. Passersby grinned and waved. Since the show had come to town, New Yorkers were ready for anything.

The apple vendor wasn't, however. The moose spotted the pushcart filled with greens and apples and bolted toward it. He ate almost as many apples as he knocked into the street. Frank paid the man for all the produce Jerry had ruined. Then he and Annie continued on their celebration ride down Fifth Avenue. Wrapped in warm blankets, they didn't feel the cold. All they could think about was the spring to come, in Europe.

Chapter Fifteen

Although it was a cold and damp morning in late March, 1887, the downtown pier was crowded — show people, reporters, animals, and passersby. Buffalo Bill's Wild West was sailing for England on a ship called the *State of Nebraska*. Carpenters had worked for days building stalls for the horses, buffalo, elk, deer, mules, and two bears.

About seventy-five Indians stood close together. There was a legend, believed by many tribes, that any Indian who crossed the big water would waste away and die. Red Shirt, chief of the performing Sioux since Sitting Bull had returned to the reservation, was talking quietly to his people.

Everywhere things were on the move. Some

animals were suspended in a sling and swung over the side of the ship. Others walked up the gangplank and were led down to the hold. Buffalo Bill, in his buckskin coat, stood with Nate Salsbury, Annie, and Frank, watching as the Deadwood coach and covered wagons rolled up the plank. Everyone was eager to get underway.

At last all were aboard and the large ship moved out of New York Harbor. It would be eighteen days before anyone saw land again. Annie headed straight for the best view. She had never seen an expanse of water like the Atlantic Ocean, and she didn't want to miss a minute of it.

A few days out to sea a terrible storm blew up. The top half of the world was filled with clapping thunder and sheets of lightning, while the bottom half was a white-capped roller coaster. Water sloshed over the deck, leaving a dangerously slippery surface. It wasn't the danger, however, that kept most people below. It was seasickness. People and animals were too nauseous to eat, too dizzy to sleep, and too weak to move. Except Annie. She was wrapped in oilskins watching the dramatic scenes from the captain's deck.

When the *State of Nebraska* finally docked in England, everyone, including Annie, was ready for dry land, ready to set up camp and give the "Old

World" a taste of the new. On exhibition grounds at the West End of London, the tents and tepees rose against the city skyline. The arena for the show would seat 30,000 people.

Queen Victoria was celebrating her Golden Jubilee — fifty years as monarch, the longest reign in English history. Royalty from many nations, as well as hundreds of thousands of tourists, were expected to fill London.

The official opening of the Wild West was set for early May, but posters announcing the show had been pasted all over London even before the *State of Nebraska* sailed into port. When a preview performance for the Prince and Princess of Wales was reviewed in the newspapers, it seemed that all of London was talking about the Wild West.

Then three days after the official opening, Queen Victoria herself asked for a command performance. She sat alone in her box, her royal court members nearby, and watched intently. After the Grand Processional entrance, she saw a prairie fire scene, stampede and roundup of buffalo, Pocahontas saving the Englishman John Smith, Custer's last battle, and cowboy and Indian racing and roping stunts.

Then Annie Oakley. In rapid succession Annie splintered glass balls, clay pigeons, and playing cards. She leapt over tables, somersaulted before shooting, and switched guns back and forth as Frank tossed up targets. Then from her table, she picked up a knife, opened it, and walked about twenty-five paces away from Frank. He held a ball attached to a string and began to whirl it around his head.

Annie turned her back to Frank, put the rifle over her shoulder, held up the knife blade in her other hand, and using it as a mirror, took aim at the swinging balls behind her. Glass shattered and the audience cheered.

The Queen leaned forward to look at this young woman even more closely. Her Majesty had said she would attend the show for only one hour, but she remained in her seat until the performance ended.

With a beckoning wave, the Queen made it known that she wished to meet some of the performers. Frank Richmond, the show announcer, introduced Buffalo Bill, who had recently been made an honorary United States colonel.

"Your Majesty, this is Colonel William F. 'Buffalo Bill' Cody." The Queen extended her hand to be kissed. She welcomed him and his entire show to England. Richmond introduced Chief Red Shirt. The Chief approached the Queen and said, "It gladdens my heart to hear words of welcome."

Then Annie was presented to the Queen, who smiled and asked her where she was born and when she had started shooting. Annie answered briefly, and then the Queen said, "You are a very, very clever little girl!"

"Thank you, Your Majesty."

That night, Annie couldn't sleep. Every time she closed her eyes, they popped open as if they had a will of their own.

"Jimmy, it's hard to believe, isn't it? Us, you and me, meeting the Queen of England, the Queen of the whole British Empire!" Then she laughed at herself. "But you know, I'm not *that* little and I am a married woman. I suppose the costume makes me look like a young girl."

"Ah, but you *are* clever!" Frank added with a smile.

Chapter Sixteen

The Queen had so enjoyed the show that she asked for another command performance, to which she invited all the foreign royalty — the Kings of Denmark and Sweden, the King and Queen of Belgium, the Kings of Saxony and Greece, the Austrian Crown Prince, the Crown Prince and Princess of Germany, the Crown Princes of Sweden and Norway, Grand Duke Michael of Russia, and a host of others. When the Deadwood stagecoach rolled across the arena, Queen Victoria knew the passengers — her son, the Prince of Wales, and four kings. Buffalo Bill was the driver.

The Russian Grand Duke was in London to become engaged to the daughter of the Prince of

Wales. The Prince was reported to be unhappy at the prospect, but had little reason to turn down the match. One morning a note was delivered to Buffalo Bill.

Col. William F. Cody
Dear Sir:
Will the little girl that shoots so cleverly in your show, shoot a match with the Grand Duke Michael of Russia?

Edward
HRH [His Royal Highness]
Prince of Wales

Cody met with John Burke, Nate Salsbury, Frank, and Annie.

"I think it's a mistake," he said.

"I think it's a great idea," Nate responded. "If you can, Annie," he said, turning to her, "shoot him off his feet!"

Burke, Cody's longtime manager and friend, agreed with Cody. "You can't do that to royalty. You've got to let him win."

"Let's not forget *we* don't have royalty," Frank said. "If Annie can beat him, she should."

Finally Annie spoke. "The papers say he's an excellent shot. If that's true, I'll have to do all I can to beat him anyway." She added, "And I'm going to try."

At ten-thirty on the morning of the match, several royal carriages arrived at the Wild West grounds. The Prince and Princess of Wales and their daughter Victoria, the Duke of Clarence, and the Russian Grand Duke with his entourage, all proceeded to the arena. Annie and Frank were waiting at the rifle table. Annie and the Grand Duke shook hands. They were each to shoot at fifty clay pigeon targets.

The Duke was tense. He missed several targets and then had a string of hits. Annie was more consistent. She swung her rifle smoothly, locating the targets with ease. Then she missed one. The Grand Duke smiled, hoping this would turn the tide. It didn't. The final score was thirty-six hits for Michael and forty-seven for Annie.

Newspaper headlines announced that the dashing Russian Duke who prided himself on his abilities with a rifle was outdone by "a little girl from Ohio." Whether the storm of publicity directly affected the Duke's marriage plans, no one can be certain. The engagement, however, was broken.

Everyone was talking about Annie. The reporters called her "Annie Oakley of the Magic Gun," and she was invited to teas and socials and shooting exhibitions. People in the street recognized her. Two shoeshine boys, spotting her across the avenue, whispered loudly, "There goes the boss shooter!"

Annie was the first woman ever to be invited to shoot at the London Gun Club. She was also the first person, man or woman, to be presented with a medal from the Club. Almost two inches in diameter, the gold medal had a view of the club on one side, and the inscription, "Presented to Miss Annie Oakley by the London Gun Club," on the other.

The Prince of Wales, who was to become Edward VII, King of England, after Queen Victoria's death, was a frequent visitor to both the Gun Club and the Wild West Show. When he saw Annie's medal, he said to her, "I know of no one so worthy of it."

Chapter Seventeen

Throughout the London tour of the Wild West Show, Annie was frequently in the headlines. She had become a big star, even bigger than in the United States.

The show finally closed in October and moved north to an indoor arena in the city of Manchester. But Annie and Frank were not with the group. Trouble had developed between Buffalo Bill and Annie. Some said Buffalo Bill was jealous that Annie was so popular. Whatever the reason, Frank and Annie decided to leave the show and travel on their own.

For several weeks they hunted at a friend's country estate outside of London. One afternoon a letter arrived for Frank. Would he and his wife care to come to Berlin, Germany, where Miss Oakley was invited to give a shooting exhibition at the request of the German Kaiser and the Crown Prince?

On a bleak November morning, they set out by train for Germany. Their hotel room was ready for them when they arrived. After a good dinner and sound sleep, they were taken the next morning to the Union-Club at Charlottenburg Racetrack. Members and friends of the Club greeted the Americans politely, but coolly. A woman shooter, indeed! The Germans loved their gun clubs. Shooting was a sport, a skill, a passion . . . for men.

They watched silently as Annie picked up a gun. Frank began tossing balls into the air. As fast as he threw them, she shattered them. Using a knife as her mirror, she shot over her shoulder at a coin Frank held between his fingers. Annie heard a low murmur of approval sweep through the viewing aisles.

Suddenly Crown Prince Wilhelm stepped into the shooting area. He walked toward the gun table, lifted one of Annie's rifles, and examined it carefully. As he replaced it in its case, he turned to her.

"Madam, in London I saw you shoot at a ciga-

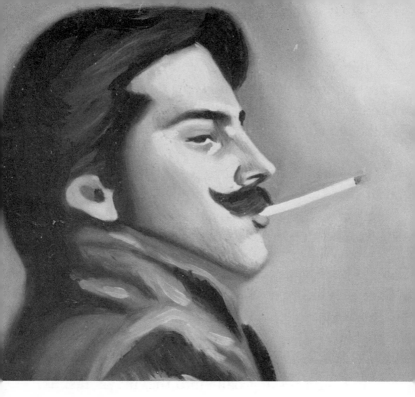

rette in the gentleman's mouth," he said gesturing
toward Frank. "Will you repeat that for us?"

"Of course," Annie replied. As she loaded her
rifle, both she and Frank were startled to see the
Crown Prince position himself at a shooting distance from her. He removed a cigarette from a
silver case, inserted it in a holder, and put it
between his lips. There was a rustling in the
audience. This man was to be the next Emperor
of Germany. Should anything happen . . . it was
unthinkable! An aide stepped forward and whis-

pered to Prince Wilhelm. The Prince shrugged him away and lit the cigarette.

Annie took aim and fired. The ash floated off the burning tip. The applause was spontaneous and strong. The Crown Prince turned to face Annie. He had a slight smile on his lips as he bowed stiffly.

That night Annie was happy but exhausted. In the quiet of their hotel room, she and Frank talked about going home. The next morning they cancelled their scheduled appearances in Paris and sailed for America. They were in New York before Christmas. While Annie rested, Frank made arrangements for new exhibitions and matches.

Over the next year Annie shot in private clubs, theaters, and public exhibitions. For one summer season, she toured with a rival Wild West show, Pawnee Bill's Frontier Exhibition. That winter she even starred in a western drama. The ads called it "The Greatest and Most Thrilling Border Drama Ever Produced — Bold Border Boys, Bad Bucking Broncos, Masterless Mexican Mustangs." And Annie. It wasn't a very good show, and it closed after a short run.

In the spring of 1889 Annie and Frank had an unexpected but welcome visitor.

"Frank, Missy, it's good to see you!" Nate Salsbury said, as he unbuttoned his overcoat. Within minutes he came straight to the point. "We miss you, Missy," he smiled. "Seriously, the Colonel and I want you back. The show is going to Paris for the Exposition celebrating the one hundredth anniversary of the French Revolution. It won't be the same without you."

Frank was tickled at the thought of the American frontier — cowboys, buffalo, Indians — in Paris. Annie was delighted at the thought of at last seeing the city. All differences forgotten, Frank and Annie rejoined Buffalo Bill's Wild West. They told Nate they felt they were coming home.

The show opened in Paris in May. As in England, it was a resounding success. After one performance a distinguished-looking black man appeared at Buffalo Bill's tent. He was introduced as the King of Senegal in West Africa. His French was fluent.

He had come on business. "I wish to buy Mademoiselle Oakley," he said.

Buffalo Bill stared at him and then chuckled. The King assured him he was absolutely serious.

"I don't own her, so I can't sell her," Cody said at last. The King increased his offer from 50,000 francs to 100,000.

"Very generous, your Majesty," said Cody, "but I'm afraid it's out of my hands. Why don't you speak to little Missy herself?"

Annie extended her hand in greeting when Cody introduced the King.

"Mademoiselle," he began. "There are wild animals threatening my villages. They are killing people. I need you and wish to buy you. You will be magnificent in helping us get rid of this problem!"

Annie was flattered, but, "Buy?" she said, astonished. Frank was enjoying the scene. Annie declined and the King insisted. Annie declined again. The King insisted again. At last he accepted her refusal.

"When he went down on his knees," she said later to Frank, "I could hardly believe what was happening."

Frank started laughing. "Wait till I tell them in North Star. They'll never believe it — an offer to buy our little Missy!"

Late in her life, Annie's collection of medals was melted down at her request. Annie sold the gold and silver and gave the money to a children's hospital.

Chapter Eighteen

The Wild West Show left France in December 1889, and sailed to Barcelona, Spain. It was a terrible time for the show. Hungry people in ragged clothes wandered the streets of the city. Children begged in groups. Even worse than the poverty was the sickness. The Americans grew to fear the sound of the wagons lurching through the streets to the burial grounds, carrying the bodies of people who had died from smallpox and influenza.

So few came to the Barcelona show that Cody and Salsbury lowered the admission price. Even so, many seats remained empty, but the fence around the arena couldn't keep the diseases out.

On Christmas Eve Frank Richmond, the show's announcer, was buried.

Barcelona was under quarantine. No one could enter or leave the city without special permission.

"We're trapped here," Annie said to Frank. "Trapped!"

"Seven of the crew have died in the last three days," Frank said. "Did Nate tell you, two more Indians have come down with smallpox?"

At the end of January the show was finally permitted to leave Spain. Deeply saddened by their friends' deaths, the crew was nevertheless cheered at the thought of going to Italy. The sunshine in Naples lifted everyones' spirits. They traveled north from Naples, performing in cities along the way.

In Paris they had marveled at the brand-new Eiffel Tower built for the Exposition. Now in Rome they stared in fascination at one of the oldest structures, the Roman Coliseum, built before the birth of Christ. Then turning a corner in Pisa, the Americans found themselves smack in front of the famous Leaning Tower. How many could climb up together, they wondered? A guide reassured them that the tower had been tilting for hundreds of years without falling down. Not everyone was comforted. The gondolas in Venice felt safer. The Americans were taken up and down the Venetian canals, Indians in feathered headdress, cowboys in Stetsons.

Just as they all felt that their problems were over, they heard disturbing news from America. It seemed there was trouble on the Indian reservations. Congress had cut the beef rations for the Indians. Crop failures had made the situation worse. The Sioux were on the verge of starvation. A new religion, inspired by a Paiute Indian named Wovoka, was spreading like a prairie fire. Wovoka prophesied the end of the white man's rule, the end of bad times for Indians.

"Do you remember," Frank said one day, "the statue of Christopher Columbus in Barcelona?" Annie nodded. He went on, "Remember the Indians saying, 'It was a bad day for us when he discovered America'?" Annie nodded again, and said, "Good for us, I guess, not so good for them."

At about this time, White Horse, an Indian with the Wild West, left the show. He told no one he was leaving or where he was going. The next anyone heard of him was in a newspaper article sent from New York City. White Horse was telling American reporters that Buffalo Bill was mistreating the Indians in his show. Cody was very upset and returned to America with a number of the Indian members of the cast to testify in Washington, D.C. The Bureau of Indian Affairs concluded that there was no problem at the Wild West Show.

But there was still a problem on the reservations. The new religion predicted that white people would die in a huge flood. All Indians who had died in the past would be reborn, and buffalo would once again roam the plains in huge herds. The religion told the Indians not to fight. Instead, they were to dance a special dance for as long and as often as they could. It was called Ghost Dancing because if you danced well enough you would see your dead ancestors.

But the Indian agents feared an uprising. And some businessmen wanted the size of the reservations reduced so that they could take over Indian lands.

When the Wild West Show closed in the fall, no one knew what was going to happen. Annie and Frank went to England to visit with friends for the winter. It was good to get away from all the bad news.

At the breakfast table one morning, their host opened the newspaper and looked up at Annie.

"I say, that's odd," he said. "It says here that you died in Buenos Aires of congestion of the lungs!"

"I died in Argentina?" Annie said. "When?"

"This past December. Look, here's a picture of you draped in black." He handed the paper to Annie. Frank looked over her shoulder.

"Remarkable!" Frank murmured.

Later they learned that a woman named Alice Oakley had died. A telegraph operator had misspelled her first name, and the newspapers had jumped on the story.

But there was a death, one that was real. One that Annie cared about. Sitting Bull had been killed at Standing Rock reservation during an attempt to arrest him. When the Chief had left the Wild West Show, Cody had given him a white show horse. Now, years later, the rifle shots that killed Sitting Bull triggered an old memory. The horse began to perform as he had in the arena. As if in an eerie dream, the horse knelt and lifted his foreleg to paw the earth as Sitting Bull lay dead nearby.

Army generals in Washington and Indian agents on the reservation had thought that Sitting Bull was a danger to the peace. Annie knew a different Sitting Bull. She remembered how he gave most of his money away to the small ragged boys who followed him around. He had never understood how people who had things didn't share with those who had little.

"The white man knows how to make everything," he had once said to Annie, "but he does not know how to distribute it."

Sitting Bull remembered his adopted daughter Annie in his will. He left her his prize possessions — his peace pipe, council stick, headdress, and the moccasins his Indian daughter had made for him to wear in the battle with Custer.

Chapter Nineteen

The Buffalo Bill Wild West Show toured Europe for nearly four years before it returned to America. Annie and Frank were ready to come home. Annie was thirty-two years old, and she and Frank decided it was time for them to live in a real house.

"Flowers and fruit trees! Oh, think of it, Jimmy. It'll be wonderful!"

They checked the newspaper ads and finally decided to buy land and build a home in Nutley, New Jersey. Both of them thought they would settle in and become homebodies whenever they weren't performing with the Wild West Show.

They tried hard. They planted a garden, made friends, joined in community activities. But they never did really settle in.

Working with Buffalo Bill meant that they still had to travel for at least seven months of the year. They became experts at making their tent a cozy home — there was always a comfortable rocker, a vase of flowers, and a brightly colored carpet on the floorboards. Visitors would sit in folding canvas chairs, or sink into plush cushions that lay on top of trunks.

At one side of the tent was Frank's travel desk, a writing table that held his papers and pens. And tucked away in a corner was a folding canvas bathtub, out of the way until its next use. In another corner sat Annie's travel trunk with four drawers, two large and two small, and a lid that tilted up to become a dresser top. Annie's sewing machine and thread and needle basket were always within easy reach. Whether in a tent, train car, or home, Annie always made curtains.

Almost everything in the tent had a story — the Indian war bonnet on the wall; the rows of medals from different cities around the world; the guns, some designed especially for Annie by famous gunmakers; the velvet cushion that Frank's dog

This trunk was made specially for Annie. The drawers were just long enough to store her short costumes without folding, and the top folded up into a dresser.

George had sat on; the photographs of Annie and Frank with their many friends from America and Europe.

The 1893 season, the year after they returned from Europe, was the most successful ever for the Wild West Show. The show set up in Chicago on fourteen acres just outside the World's Fair grounds. Annie and Frank planted flowers around their tent.

The show had a new name — Buffalo Bill's Wild West and Congress of Rough Riders of the World. Riders and soldiers from different countries performed for the American audiences. Arabs raced against Russian Cossacks and Mexicans. Cavalry from England, France, and Germany paraded and performed stunts. It was as if the Wild West were putting on a world's fair of its own. The expanded show included all the regular acts — the ambush of the emigrant train and Deadwood Stagecoach, the ride of the pony express, the buffalo roundup, the attack on the settlers' cabin.

It rained steadily during the first weeks of the show, but no one paid much attention. The Wild West performers went on, rain or shine. Annie stood on bales of straw as she changed costumes to keep from getting mud on her skirt hems. Once dressed, she paid little attention to the weather.

The stands held 18,000 people and quickly filled to capacity. The audience didn't seem to care about the rain, either.

Johnny Baker was another sharpshooter with the show. As a young teenager, he'd idolized Buffalo Bill and had come to work as a stagehand. He'd been learning to shoot, and when Annie joined the show, she also taught him some tricks. Johnny developed into an excellent shot. Sometimes he and Annie staged a shooting match between them. Reporters often asked him if he was "just letting the lady win." Johnny said, "There never was a day when I didn't try to beat her, but it just couldn't be done." Most people he shot against become nervous or distracted, he added, but not Annie Oakley.

At the end of the Chicago tour, Annie and Frank went back to their home in Nutley. They'd been away so long, some birds had built a nest in the chimney in the dining room. Smoke backed up into the room whenever they lit the fire. Frank reached for a gun and shot up the chimney. Soot came flying down, settling all over the room. Annie looked at Frank.

"Maybe this is telling us something. Maybe we're not meant to be home folks."

"I know what you mean," Frank said. "I had the

same thought when I realized we hadn't built any closets."

They both laughed. No closets! Then Annie said, "It feels like we start packing again even before everything's unpacked. It's faster to leave things neatly in trunks."

When she thought about it, Annie said to herself, I guess you just can't cage a gypsy.

Within a short time, Frank and Annie began to rent out the house. Several years later, they sold it. They were happier on the move, putting down stakes and then picking up and moving on.

Chapter Twenty

Annie and Frank loved visiting with Annie's family in Ohio during the winter months. Annie sometimes sent her mother fruit trees for planting in the spring. When she and Frank arrived at the old homestead, Mrs. Shaw would be putting up jellies and preserves from "Annie's fruits." Annie would sit in the kitchen with her mother, talking, listening, and mending her costumes. Frank would wander down to the general store and sit for hours with the neighbors, listening to local news and telling stories of his and Annie's days on the road.

Both Annie and Frank spent time with nieces, nephews, and their young friends. Frank would make up poems and jokes for the children. Annie would play paper games. She'd tear up small pieces, wet them, and paste them on her eyelids, cheeks, nose, and chin. Then as everyone giggled she'd make faces and sounds, pretending to be strange creatures. These outings were always fun for Annie and Frank. It was a relaxing time, no schedules, no packing and unpacking, no "have-to's."

Annie's family loved the show stories, but they had never seen her actually perform. Independence Day, July 4, 1896, was their first chance. Buffalo Bill's Wild West Show was coming to Piqua, a town some thirty miles from their home.

Posters on all the barn walls showed pictures of Buffalo Bill and Annie. She was called "The Peerless Wing and Rifle Shot," and "The Champion Shot of the World." Annie never liked the word "champion." People were always challenging you to a match if you were a "champion." She just wanted to be the best she could. But others wanted to call her a champion, and they did.

Those posters were exciting for all her relatives and friends. Someone famous, someone they knew. And that person was coming to town to perform!

On the day of the show, Annie's mother arrived in her Quaker dress. Her sisters, brother John, and all their children were also there. Annie took them on a special tour of the grounds. They got to see the ammunition wagon, where bullet shells were loaded before the show. They were introduced to anyone they thought was interesting, like the blacksmiths, and the cooks who prepared food for nearly four hundred people. But the best part was when Annie waved to their section of the grandstand as she rode into the arena.

There was another first for Annie that year. In the fall, the show traveled to Sioux Falls, South Dakota, and "The Little Maid of the Western Plains" saw those plains for the first time. The real Annie Oakley and the theater Annie Oakley had both come home.

Chapter Twenty-one

Over the next years, Annie and Frank traveled throughout the country on long trains filled with performers, animals, scenery, and equipment.

In 1901 the show toured through the Midwest and the South. It had been a hot and humid summer, and Annie and Frank were tired. They talked about retiring, and even considered settling down once again.

On October 28, the show played to an enthusiastic crowd in Charlotte, North Carolina. By midnight everything was loaded on the trains, and they were headed north for Danville, Virginia. It was to be the last show of the season.

The show train was divided into three sections

that were traveling separately. The engineer of a southbound freight traveling in the opposite direction pulled over to a railroad siding to let the show train pass. It was only the first section, but he didn't realize that. After it had passed, he moved his train back onto the main track. At 3:20 A.M. he suddenly saw the lights of the second section rapidly approaching him. Neither he nor the engineer of the show train was able to stop in time. A whistle pierced the night.

Annie and Frank were in their bunks asleep. Suddenly the air was filled with the awful cries of screaming animals. Miraculously no people died, but over one hundred horses were killed or had to be shot. Old Pap, one of Buffalo Bill's favorite horses, was one of them.

"Annie, where are you?" Frank shouted.

"I'm okay. It's all right, Jimmy, I'm okay."

Frank groped through the darkness in the car until he found her. They climbed over trunks and boxes and made their way through the wreckage to the siding where Buffalo Bill was standing. Annie's back hurt a little. She felt some pain when she turned or bent over.

"Just bruises, no wounds," she said as she looked over her arms and legs. The same was true for Frank and Cody.

It was hard to get out of bed in the days that followed. Nothing seemed to be wrong, but Annie needed a rest. She decided to go to a health spa to soak in the hot mineral baths. She thought that would rid her of all her aches. But an attendant made a terrible mistake and left her in a steaming bath for forty minutes instead of the usual two.

Shortly after the train accident and the experience at the baths, Annie awakened one morning and went into the bathroom. As she looked in the mirror, she caught her breath.

"Jimmy, good Lord, Jimmy, come quick!" Her hand reached up to touch her long, chestnut-colored hair. It had turned completely white. Annie was a white-haired lady at age forty-one.

A few days later, a brief announcement was printed in the newspapers. Annie Oakley was leaving Buffalo Bill's Wild West Show. She had performed with the show for seventeen good years. It was time now to move on.

Chapter Twenty-two

At first no one thought Annie had been seriously hurt in the train crash. Within months, however, she entered St. Michael's Hospital in Newark, New Jersey, with internal injuries, and had to have several operations. Doctors predicted she'd never perform again. But Annie had earned money shooting since age thirteen, and she wasn't about to stop now.

After Annie came out of the hospital and recovered, a well-known playwright, Langdon McCormick, wrote a drama especially for her to star in. It was called *The Western Girl*. She played a character named Nance Barry who roped, rode, and shot. In the final scene, Annie saved the lieutenant she loved by lassoing the woman who was about to stab him. The newspaper reviewers said the star shooter had become a shooting star. Annie Oakley was conquering the theater just as she had conquered every other arena she had played in.

During the second act one night, Annie came on stage on horseback as usual. But this night her horse, Bess, was spooked by something and unexpectedly jumped and bucked. Annie was thrown against the stage set. The curtain quickly closed and a stagehand rushed out.

"Is there a doctor in the house?" he yelled.

Dr. Guion was in the audience. He left his seat and rushed backstage. Annie had been hit on the bridge of her nose and was stunned. But within a short time she went back onstage to finish the act.

Annie performed in *The Western Girl* for nearly six months. When the play finally closed, Frank arranged exhibitions and matches for her. One morning as Annie and Frank were finishing breakfast, the mail arrived with a fat envelope for Annie. When she opened it, there was a note from a friend and several newspaper clippings. The headlines were astonishing.

Annie made her stage debut in *The Western Girl*. It was a big hit.

"Annie Oakley, Famous Rifle Shot, In Jail"

"Annie Oakley's Downfall!"

*"Annie Oakley Steals Man's Trousers
Sells them to Buy Morphine"*

Robbery, drugs, jail! Annie and Frank couldn't believe what they were reading. A woman in Chicago had been arrested, and the newspapers claimed she was Annie.

> *Annie Oakley is a prisoner in the Harrison Street Police Court. She pleaded guilty and was fined $25. According to the police, the woman is addicted to the use of drugs. She was formerly with Buffalo Bill's show and commanded the salary of a light opera prima donna, was petted and fêted and awarded honors at meetings of fashionable gun clubs.*

"How can they make up things like that about me?" Annie cried. "If people believe this, I may never be able to work again."

"It'll be all right," Frank said. "I can earn enough money for both of us, and we'll spend what we have to, to get your good name back."

Annie wrote to several newspapers saying that a dreadful mistake had been made. She was in New Jersey, she had never been arrested, and she had never taken drugs. The woman in Chicago was an imposter. After several days two papers printed apologies, but others continued to publish the story.

Annie and Frank hired a lawyer. Annie was so upset, she had trouble sleeping and eating. Her name, her good name, meant everything.

"What if someone believes these stories and won't hire Annie?" Frank asked the lawyer.

"We will sue these newspapers," he answered. "This is libel. When they publish untrue stories, and they don't check them out, and you suffer, well, that's libel. And we will sue them for thousands of dollars."

"I don't care about the money," Annie said. "It's the idea that people are reading these terrible lies about me — it's more than I can stand. I have to fight it."

For three years Annie and Frank did fight. They spent a good deal of time in courtrooms all around the country. They sued over fifty newspapers, and as each case came to trial Annie testified in court. People packed into the courtrooms to get a glimpse of "the world's champion rifle shot." When she

117

was called to the stand, Annie told of her travels with the Buffalo Bill Wild West Show and her theater performances and exhibition matches.

In many of the cases, the newspapers admitted that the articles were wrong, but they argued that Annie shouldn't get much money because she was only suing, they said, for the publicity.

At home Annie said to Frank, "Publicity! They have the nerve to say I want this kind of publicity!"

Annie got publicity of another kind as well. "It's been hard being a woman professional shooter," she said one day to Frank. "Nobody expected me to be able to shoot and I showed I could. But these articles," she said as she flung one aside, "they spend more time talking about my being a woman than about the case."

Annie picked up another one and read: " 'Her voice has no tinge of masculinity and has the soft musical ring of the usual voice of the weaker sex.' Can you imagine, 'the weaker sex'!"

Annie won case after case and was awarded thousands of dollars. In the end, however, she wasn't able to keep much of the money because the trials had cost so much. And she was never exuberant after winning. She felt that the newspapers had been terribly irresponsible. They hadn't taken the time to check the story. They hadn't even written that the woman *claimed* to be Annie Oakley. They said she *was* Annie Oakley. Well, now they had heard from the real Annie Oakley, and they weren't likely to forget it.

Chapter Twenty-three

Annie went back to doing what she did best — showing her remarkable skills as a shooter. Thousands saw her as she and Frank toured the country giving exhibitions. Many of the shows were free to the public, for Annie and Frank were demonstrating ammunition and guns made by two companies.

Annie was back in the headlines, but this time it was the real Annie.

"Annie Oakley Thrills Crowd"

"Remarkable Crack Shot"

"Best of Her Line in the World"

One evening Annie and Frank watched the act of another woman shooter, Winona. Winona performed from a high-flying trapeze, hanging by her knees as she fired at a target. When she hit the bull's-eye, a bell rang. Annie offered to let Winona use some of her targets.

"Heavens, no!" the woman exclaimed. "To tell the truth, I hardly know one end of the rifle from the other. It's blanks I'm using. The property man rings the bell after I shoot."

Later Frank reminded Annie of a time in France when a person in the audience had challenged Annie to prove that she was really hitting the targets.

"Remember that very properly dressed man?" he asked. "Took out his pocket watch, like a fool, and offered it as a target."

"Most of all," Annie said, laughing, "I remember his face when you whirled it around for me and smash! — the only thing left was a tiny inner spring."

There was no mistaking Annie's ability. Her trick of shooting nearly a dozen holes in a playing card tossed in the air was so famous that everyone knew about it. Anyone who picked up one of these cards after the show was allowed in free the next time.

There is a story that Ban Johnson, the president of American League baseball, was shown the season pass of a man who had used it so often it was filled with holes. Johnson said, "It looks as though Annie Oakley's been shooting at it!" The phrase stuck, and the name "Annie Oakley" came to mean a free ticket. The term is still in many dictionaries today.

Annie had done just about everything she could in show business — circuses, Wild West shows, stage performances, exhibitions, matches, demonstrations. Now it was time for something new. On one of their trips to North Carolina for the winter, both Annie and Frank joined the Carolina Hotel staff in Pinehurst, offering shooting lessons for women and men.

For Annie, teaching began when one day she overheard a woman in the Carolina Hotel lobby. "My, how I wish I were a man so that I could shoot! I think it must be splendid to be able to fire a gun and hit something."

Annie introduced herself and said, "I've always believed that outside of heavy labor, anything a man can do a woman can also do. And this is certainly true of firearms." She offered to show them, and the next morning the woman came to the rifle range with two friends, all anxious to begin.

They did no shooting that first day. Annie taught them the careful use of a gun. "Never point it at anyone or anything you're not planning to shoot." Frank had always said the same thing to children, showing them how to handle toy guns.

"Start with the right habits, and you'll be safe all your life," he'd say.

Annie was a practical person and a practical teacher. Whenever her students asked which was the best gun, she'd say, "There's no such thing. The best gun is the one that fits you." By the time Annie left Pinehurst, she had taught nearly 15,000 women to shoot.

Many famous people came to the Carolina and shot with Frank and Annie — John D. Rockefeller, the millionaire industrialist, Will Rogers, the "Cowboy Philosopher" and newspaper columnist, Warren Harding, the senator and later President of the United States. Some, like Will Rogers, remained friends for life.

Chapter Twenty-four

World War I began in 1914, and the German Kaiser, who had declared war on Russia and France, was the very one whose cigarette ashes Annie had sent flying.

"Too bad you were such a good shot," the newspaper reporters teased Annie.

"I could always ask for a rematch," she replied.

When America finally joined the allies in the war against Germany and Austria, Annie wrote to the War Department and offered her services as a shooting instructor. A low-level officer read the letter, said, "We don't need women," and rejected her offer. But Annie kept trying. Finally, senior officers agreed that demonstrations by crack shot Annie Oakley would be good for the soldiers to see. And so at their own expense, refusing to take any money from the government, Annie and Frank toured army bases and gave exhibitions.

One afternoon at a demonstration at Camp Crane in Pennsylvania, Annie had the soldiers gaping in astonishment. She sat in a chair, leaned back and with the rifle over her shoulder shot coins, marbles, and cards. Frank and Annie had a new dog, Dave, and he sat patiently as apples flew off his head. The soldiers gathered around to talk with Annie and Frank after the demonstration.

"If Uncle Sam had one regiment of crack shots like you, they would clean up the German Army," one soldier said admiringly.

Even Dave joined the war effort. Annie, Frank, and Dave raised money for the Red Cross. Spectators at exhibitions were asked to give some money to be wrapped in a handkerchief or piece of paper. Dave was allowed to smell the money and then, while he was blindfolded, it was hidden within a hundred yards of his stand. If he found the money, it would be donated to the Red Cross. Dave had a wonderful nose, and often

Annie with her husband, Frank Butler, and their beloved dog, Dave, at Pinehurst, North Carolina.

raised more than a thousand dollars in one afternoon. The Red Cross ran advertisements with Dave's picture in newspapers around the country. If he can work for the war effort, so can you! the ads said.

Chapter Twenty-five

Several years after the war, Annie and Frank were riding with friends in Florida, when the car they were in swerved to avoid a collision and overturned. Annie was rushed to the hospital with a broken hip. Her ankle was so badly injured, she had to wear a brace on her right leg for the rest of her life.

Annie was older, and her recovery took longer than with past injuries. Usually a cheerful person, she became depressed and thought she didn't have long to live.

"Jimmy, I want to find all my medals," she said one day.

"That's a lot of cartons to go through, Annie," he said.

"It doesn't matter. I want them." When they gathered all her medals together, Annie had them melted down. She sold the gold and silver and gave the money to a children's hospital.

That was very like her. If she read an article in the newspaper about people in trouble, she would often send money to the paper. She'd enclose a note saying that the money was ten percent of her earnings from a recent exhibition, and to please forward it to the needy family.

It was hard for Annie to stay depressed for long. Soon she was again giving exhibitions, but she tired easily. Her last public appearance was in 1925. After that, Annie and Frank went to live with relatives and friends in Ohio.

Her old friend Will Rogers visited with Annie and wrote a newspaper column about her. It was printed in papers all across the country:

I went out to see Annie Oakley the other day . . . in Dayton, Ohio. She lives there with her husband, Frank Butler, and her sister. Her hair is snow-white. She is bedridden from an auto accident a few years ago. I have talked with Buffalo Bill cowboys who were with the show for years and they worshipped her . . . I want you to write her, all of you who remember her, and those that can, go see her. Her address is 706 Lexington Avenue, Dayton, Ohio. She will be a lesson to you. She is a greater character than she was a rifle shot.

The letters poured in. People wrote to tell her how thrilled they had been as children to see her perform. *Should my brothers wander away when we were at the show*, one woman wrote, *Dad would say don't worry, we will find them over where the lady shooter is.*

Annie answered all of the mail. Then she began to give away her treasures. At last, on November 3, 1926, she died.

Annie, who had been so much a part of Frank's life, Annie, whom he had loved so, was gone. Within two weeks, sick and lonely, he too died. They were buried together on Thanksgiving day, exactly fifty-one years after they had met and fallen in love. Their tombstones sit side by side: Annie Oakley, 1926, at rest; Frank E. Butler, 1926 at rest.

Postscript

Annie Oakley was so famous a person that years after she died movies and shows were written about her life. There was even a television series about her. *Annie Get Your Gun* is the most famous musical show about Annie. There is, however, a mystery about these movies and shows. They don't tell the real story of Annie Oakley, even though the truth was known. Why?

In the movies and shows about Annie, she lets Frank beat her at shooting. Perhaps the writers thought that an audience would never like the story of a girl who beat a famous man sharpshooter. But Annie did beat him. She wouldn't throw a match to the Russian Grand Duke, let alone Frank Butler!

The writers also seemed to believe that no man would marry a woman who beat him in a shooting match. But Frank not only loved Annie for who she was, he also gave up his own shooting career to manage hers. Frank was more interesting than the writers pictured him, and Annie was true to herself.

In the end, the real story is the best story.

Step Back in Time With
SCHOLASTIC BIOGRAPHY

☐ **40639-6 The Death of Lincoln: A Picture History of the Assassination**
The sad and chilling story of Lincoln's death, and what happened afterward.

☐ **40512-8 The Defenders**
The tragic stories of three American Indian heroes.

☐ **40933-6 The First Woman Doctor**
A woman doctor was unheard of in 1840. But Elizabeth Blackwell followed her dream and became the *first*.

☐ **42218-9 Frederick Douglass Fights for Freedom**
The moving story of Frederick Douglass, a former slave who fought for the freedom and equality of his people.

☐ **40640-X Freedom Train: The Story of Harriet Tubman**
Harriet Tubman escaped slavery, but never forgot her people. She risked her life daily to help hundreds of others to freedom.

☐ **41024-5 Great Escapes of World War II**
Seven true stories of daring escapes by prisoners of war during World War II.

☐ **41344-9 John Fitzgerald Kennedy: America's 35th President**
Follows the life of John F. Kennedy and highlights the memorable events of his presidency.

☐ **41711-8 Pocahontas and the Strangers**
The story of the Indian princess who risked her life to bring peace between the Indians and the English.

☐ **41183-7 Secret Missions: Four True-Life Stories**
Details of the exciting and sometimes dangerous lives of four courageous people!

☐ **41342-2 They Led the Way: Fourteen American Women**
The first woman to run for president…a freed slave who wrote poetry… these great women made history—by doing just what they wanted to do!

☐ **40488-1 The Wright Brothers at Kitty Hawk**
Orville and Wilbur Wright had a dream that one day men would fly. On December 17, 1903, their dream came true!

PREFIX CODE 0-590

Available wherever you buy books, or use the coupon below. $2.50 each.